T0113616

I HAD MY CAKE and ATE IT TOO

THANKS TO MY ANGELS

T ERRENCE B OYLE

Archway Publishing books may be ordered through booksellers or by contacting:

Archway Publishing
1663 Liberty Drive
Bloomington, IN 47403
www.archwaypublishing.com
844-669-3957

ISBN: 978-1-6657-0377-2 (sc)
ISBN: 978-1-6657-0378-9 (e)

Library of Congress Control Number: 2021904139

Print information available on the last page.

Archway Publishing rev. date: 03/05/2021

Contents

Preface

I found in life that angels do in fact exist! Not as flying people with wings, but as everyday people who come into your life, help you in some way, never ask for anything in return, and then leave in the same quiet way they came. I have had many such angels in my life. Although I did not know it at the time, they helped me a great deal, and I will forever be grateful.

To be sure, there were some bumps along the way. But as I look back, I can see that they all helped me to grow. After all, it is not whether or not you have problems but how you handle them.

This story is about my journey through life.

Chapter 1

ANGEL NUMBER 1, MOM

I have to say, my mom was my first angel. She formed my character and the type of person I am today, for which I thank her. I learned a great deal from her, including manners; how to fix things (she was very pragmatic); and how to sew and iron. Although she left school in the third grade, she could read, write, and speak fluent German as a second language. My head is filled with what one of my IBM colleagues called "Boyle witticisms," which Mom passed on to us. They include the following classics:

- "Don't be like them; be yourself."
- "Turn the other cheek."
- "There but for the grace of God go I."

My earliest recollection is rather surreal. We were moving to a house on Ogden Avenue in Jersey City, New Jersey, in 1944. I was seven years old. I observed myself walking north on the east side of the street while I was actually walking across the street on the west side. Perhaps a strange out-of-body experience? It seems I was reincarnated, since I have no recollection of life before that. I have no idea how we moved to our home on Ogden Avenue.

The house had been vacant for a long time, judging from how

dirty it was, with dust all over the place. I entered the kitchen and saw a wood-burning Franklin stove with a shelf above the burners. On that shelf was a hand grenade. It fell to the floor, fortunately not armed.

The backyard was filled with weeds and brush. There were four wooden sheds, and we found a trunk in one of them. When we opened the trunk, there was a white violin inside. We picked it up, and it fell apart.

My mom had bought the house for back taxes of $2,400, which she borrowed from my brother Sunny Jim, who had just returned from service in the navy aboard the USS *Enterprise*. He'd won the money gambling on board. Sunny was aboard the *Enterprise* at Pearl Harbor when it was attacked. He lost most of the friends who were stationed with him. I was only four years old at the time. I found out later that it took a week for our family to find out whether Sunny was dead or alive.

The house was a four-story Victorian (with a ground-floor basement, first, second, and third floors), built in 1892 for $2,000. I searched the town records for a mortgage but only found a loan taken out for the land. It had fourteen rooms, which worked for us as a large family of nine children. Mom was a hard worker, and together we put the house in shape before too long. It always amazed me how Mom, since she had to work and never went beyond the third grade in school, had so much knowledge. She could do anything, including all repairs to the house—fixing the roof, coating shingles with creosote, painting, putting up screens, and so on.

Mom was a Protestant, but she made sure all of us went to Mass every Sunday, and she gave us each a nickel for the collection basket. My father was an Irish Catholic but was not involved in our upbringing. He just worked, providing an income. Every week, Mom sent me to where Pop worked to collect the pay (ninety-four dollars, I believe). She gave me bus fare to make the journey of about three miles round trip.

The house had no heat except for the wood-burning stove in

the kitchen and kerosene stoves in the hallway on each of the three landings. In the winter, I slept with socks on my hands and feet, bundled up in pajamas and a bathrobe, and with flannel top and bottom sheets on my bed.

Mom was very outgoing and made friends quickly. Our neighbors often came knocking on our door, asking Mom to help a plant that was ailing. She always brought it back to life. Mom had the richest soil in town, which she shared with whomever needed help with their plants. I helped enrich the soil by following the horse and wagon that came by every day with fruits and vegetables. The horse gave willingly, and I accepted his "gifts" with my dustpan and bucket. It gave my friends lots of ammunition to make fun of me, but not too often.

Nothing went to waste with Mom. Cigarette ashes, ashes from the stove (after *clinkers*, unburned coals, were removed), waste vegetable matter, and so on went into the compost heap, which would later be spread around the garden. She even had cord strung above the garden on which she tied old screws and nails, which would drip rust into the soil. Talk about recycling—Mom invented it!

Holidays were special. Mom, who was very artistic, always decorated. My mom was Prussian and German, so Christmas always meant a real fir tree big enough to reach the nine-foot ceiling, which Mom and the boys found and carried home. We had a set of Lionel trains and numerous decorations that Mom always set up. She made sprays and snow blocks—Styrofoam bases with miniature snow scenes on top—which she also made for neighbors.

Christmas dinner was always full of family around the dining room table under the Tiffany chandelier (had to be a real Tiffany, since it came with the house). Mom was not a great cook—there was lots of frying and Crisco—but could she bake! Strudels, pies, puddings, and cakes were all around the dining room, wherever there was space. Easter was the same. Mom always made a basket for each child, regardless of age. I remember her counting out jelly beans, not only by number but also by color. She must have been a little compulsive.

Chapter 2

EARLY TEENS

As a child in the city, we were never at a loss for something to do. We had a hill that ran from the easternmost block in Jersey City to Hoboken, ninety feet below us, to Paterson Plank Road, which started in Hoboken. We lived in what was called Jersey City Heights, the beginning of the Palisades. To get to Hoboken, you walked down 120 steps or the switchback Mountain Road, which was paved with cobblestones to provide traction for horses before cars replaced them. It also provided the neighborhood kids with an unbelievable snow ride on our Radio Flyer sleds: two switchbacks for a total ride of about one thousand feet.

That hill provided us many hours of entertainment. Back then, we always had plenty of snow. If you made it all the way without stopping, you got the ride of your life. We even built our own snowbank at the end of the second switchback to negotiate the turn without stopping. It was impossible for cars to negotiate that hill unless they had chains on their tires. That made it safer for us, since traffic was always light. We would then climb the 120 steps back up to the beginning of the hill and fly down again. What a life!

Many years later, Jersey City negotiated with a contractor to pave Mountain Road in exchange for the cobblestones (eighteen-inch

Belgian blocks, quite expensive). The city also made the road one-way, going up.

There was a tree that grew at a forty-five-degree angle over the edge of the cliff. Someone tied a strong rope to a branch that protruded over the cliff. We would grab the rope, back up a bit, and swing out over the cliff. Ninety feet below was the Koven Boiler Works, where they manufactured iron hot-water boilers (this was before the glass-lined boilers we use today). At the bottom of the cliff was Koven's yard, where they had a tank that looked like a horse's water trough. It was filled with something they used to clean the boilers. From the top of the cliff to the bottom were two concrete ledges. The first was thirty feet down and the second thirty feet lower, and thirty feet below that was Koven's concrete floor.

One day, one of our friends reached for the rope and missed it. He fell to the bottom, bouncing off the two ledges on the way down and landing a few feet from that cleaning liquid. He got up, walked up the 120 steps, and went home. The tree was directly behind the apartment building where he lived. All he suffered was a cracked rib and two chipped front teeth!

I visited the site recently to see if the tree was still there. I found that the path we took to that tree was blocked by a high concrete wall. That path was about four blocks long and bordered the Palisades, without a railing or fence, which was probably why it was blocked off.

Another favorite pastime we enjoyed was a wooden trolley trestle that ran from Ogden Avenue (where I lived) to Washington Street in Hoboken. Below the trestle was a steel cable that ran about two hundred feet from Ogden to the bottom of the hill at a height of about ninety feet. There was a Public Service electric transfer station on Ogden Avenue, across the street from where the trolley started its journey to Hoboken. They had a cyclone fence on Ogden, which we scaled to get U-shaped steel brackets with a porcelain roller on a steel pin. These were used to suspend electric cables on telephone poles.

We would remove the steel pin and the roller and reassemble it on the steel cable under the trestle. Then one of us would grab onto the bracket and ride the cable down to Hoboken. Top that, Tom Sawyer! Never a dull moment in my childhood. What a ride! And we did not have to pay for it or wait in line.

Sometimes we walked the trestle to the Fabian Theater on Washington Street in Hoboken. In the summer we walked to the Hudson River by the Lincoln Tunnel, about a three-mile walk. On the way, we would stop off at an empty lot and collect discarded soda bottles; there was a two-cent refund for returned empties. We collected enough to buy some pretzel rods and a Coke each. That was our lunch. Sometimes there was enough left over to buy some loosies—at that time, we could buy a single cigarette for two cents or three for a nickel—which we sometimes shared.

There were some obsolete wooden barges stored in the Hudson near the Lincoln Tunnel. Someone tied a rope to the last one, which dangled into the Hudson. At first, I didn't know how to swim, so I would dive in toward the rope and grab it. At that time, all of us were weight lifters, so it was not hard to climb the rope. Once I overran the rope and almost got caught in the current, which would have carried me to the narrows. Luckily, I made it to the rope.

Some people used the Hudson as a dumping ground, so it was dangerous where we dove. There was a case of a boy diving in and getting his head caught in an old milk can (milk cans were about three feet long and had a large opening—large enough for a head to enter). I heard the boy died.

Then we graduated to weight lifting in a friend's basement. We bought our weights for ten cents a pound from Joe Weider's original store, an old wooden building on Concorde Street in Jersey City. Working for Joe was an African American man named Leroy Colbert—the first man to develop a twenty-one-inch arm. He is in the Body Building Hall of Fame for doing so. This man was a sight to see riding down the block on his full-size '74 Harley Davidson motorcycle, lighted like a Christmas tree, wearing his black motorcycle jacket filled with studs, with his black leather cap (think Marlin Brando) and V-shaped figure. Leroy Colbert can still be found on the internet.

Besides getting our weights from Joe Weider, I also "borrowed" a few window-sash weights from my mom's house, where I lived. We tied a rope through the holes in the weights, strung the rope through a pulley nailed to a ceiling joist in the basement, and tied the other end of the rope to a broomstick. That was our last pull-down.

I was attending Dickenson High School in Jersey City, enrolled in the industrial course, taking woodworking, drafting, etc. I made a five-foot-long, one-and-a-half-inch-thick solid oak bench for bench-pressing (I paid for the wood). I carried that bench, which was quite heavy, from school to the basement where we worked out, fourteen blocks away. I was too young to drive, and it would not have fit on a bus. We worked out for about three years in the basement. Somehow, we all managed to develop well-toned muscles, and it kept us out of trouble.

I found a part-time job with Dave Halpern, who owned a linoleum store in our neighborhood. Dave was a very nice man who was generous with me. Also, since I was lifting weights, I was strong enough to handle full rolls of linoleum. Often, Mom would have me pick up linoleum for the house, which she would install with my help.

Dave hired Fred, a local man who had a pickup truck, to deliver linoleum. Fred would pay me to help him. At night, there were a few times I "borrowed" Fred's truck for a joyride (instead of a key, there were two wires hanging down from the dashboard that you twisted). I think the truck was a 1949 Ford, really beat-up, with a floor starter and floor shift. It was where I learned to drive. Somehow, I always managed to get the same spot to park in from where I started. If Fred knew, he never mentioned it.

Sometimes I would play hooky from school and join Fred to drive to a home he had built in Chester, New Jersey. We would stop at a general store and pick up a loaf of bread and some cold cuts and drinks for lunch.

One March, I brought my bathing suit for a dip in a nearby mountain stream. When I walked into the stream, I felt like I was standing in a bucket of ice. It had never occurred to me that the water would be so cold, but hey, it *was* a mountain stream.

Fred was a good guy but had several medical issues. I always had a way to earn some money, in my early teens. Once, on our way to Chester, Fred and I came upon a trucker who had lost his load of sheet metal, probably due to a bad turn. Fred stopped to help him. While loading the sheet metal onto the truck, one of them must have snagged forty dollars from my watch pocket, which Fred had received for payment on a delivery we had just completed and which I was holding. Never realized it until later!

Chapter 3

ANGEL NUMBER 2, JANET

We used to hang out in a sweet shop called Jan's Luncheonette. In the spring of 1955, when I was seventeen-and-a-half years old, most of my friends decided to join the Marines. I was attending Dickenson High School in Jersey City at the time, from January 1952 to June 1955. It was at that time I met my first wife, Janet, who had just started working as a waitress at Jan's Luncheonette (no relation to owner).

Janet was separated from and on her way to divorcing her husband. We started dating. I quit high school in the back half of the tenth year and got a job in a fluorescent-lamp factory, Duro Test. Janet taught me how to grow up (she was twenty-nine years old when we met and I was seventeen). We dated for four years until I was twenty-one—old enough to marry without my parents' consent. My mom tried in vain to break us up, but to no avail.

I lived at home, in Mom's house, until Janet and I were married. After that, Mom softened up, especially after we had a boy and a girl whom Mom loved very much. Janet and I saved for those four years and paid for our own catered-affair wedding, inviting two hundred people. We also had all our furniture paid off and went on vacation to Miami, Florida.

Chapter 4

ANGEL NUMBER 3, JOHN A.

Janet got me a job with her cousin John, who owned an auto repair shop. John's business was mainly trucks, so sometimes we had to repair them in the yard. One year, it was so cold working in that yard that I had to use two creepers: one to lie on and one to block the wind. Tools would stick to my hands, it was so cold. I would go from a cold house to a cold garage and cold work, then return to a cold house.

One day, while I was eating my lunch, John tossed me a brochure for Lincoln Technical Institute and said, "Here, do something with your life! Go to school!" I got a GED diploma with a high enough mark to get into college. I needed the diploma to go to a technical school. I signed up to learn how to rebuild automatic transmissions. I paid over eight hundred dollars for six months of training. I rebuilt a few at John's garage—not too successfully!

On my twenty-second birthday, December 16, 1959, I was using a pneumatic hammer to remove a kingpin from a truck axle when a small piece of steel, the size of half a sequin, broke off and went into my left eye. I saw a spark and immediately closed my eyes, but it was too late. I went into the office to look in the mirror. I noticed a slight scratch on the edge of both my upper and lower left eyelids at the same point. I also noticed a small cut in my iris at that point. I then started seeing bubbles floating in my left eye, sort of like kaleidoscope patterns in shades of gray. There were exactly thirteen of them.

I went to Jersey City Medical Center, where fortunately for me, Dr. Francis X. Brophy was practicing. He took X-rays and saw the steel one-quarter of an inch short of my optic nerve in my left eye. Using a large magnetic machine, Dr. Brophy removed the steel, following the path by which the steel had entered. He would ask me, while trying to remove the steel, if I felt pain (which would mean he had to change direction). He was successful and stitched the wound caused by the steel.

Two weeks later, Dr. Brophy removed the cataract caused by the steel that went through the lens in my left eye. I had to wear a hard contact lens, which became a problem. At that time, there were three types of lenses that I knew of: hard, permeable, and soft. I was restricted to the hard lens, since I had astigmatism (an imperfection in the curvature of the cornea) in that eye. Wearing a hard lens was like having a permanent eyelash in your eye. Some people were able to get used to it, but I could not.

One of the disadvantages of being an auto mechanic was that we had to work under cars and sometimes rust and dirt would get into our eyes. I would have to jump up and wash my hands in a solvent and then in soap and water before I could remove the lens from my eye, which was by then tearing badly. I gave up wearing the lens, which, while it was problematic, at least gave me dimensional vision. Without the lens, I wore an eyepatch. Without the patch, I had double vision for twenty-eight years, since Dr. Brophy did not think lens implants were perfected yet.

Twenty-eight years later, after Dr. Brophy passed away, his son, also an eye surgeon, installed an implant in my eye, which gave me 20/40 vision without glasses and no more double vision or loss of depth perception. Since John had employee compensation, I was awarded 200 percent loss of vision in my left eye, which amounted to $7,700 dollars: $35 per week for two hundred weeks. I used the money to buy our first house for $6,000.

My wife was pregnant when I got hurt. It bothered her a lot. She went to term and was having a rough time; she spent many hours in delivery. The doctor decided to perform a cesarean section (the old way, top to bottom of her stomach). Sadly, the baby was born a blue baby (congenital heart failure). The doctor, without thinking, whispered the baby's condition to me within earshot of my wife. Then, he told me not to tell her (brilliant), or she might burst her stitches. The doctor told her the baby was having difficulty and had to stay in the incubator. I had to arrange a funeral and bury the baby myself, without telling my wife.

Also, soon after my eye injury, John let me go, stating I was costing him money. Glad he gave me the brochure! As it turned out, I had to have that accident to leave John's for my life's journey. While I still have problems with that eye, it was worth it to get out of that job. Janet and I went on to have two children in 1961 and 1963, a girl and a boy, and both were born healthy.

Chapter 5

ANGEL NUMBER 4, STEVE P.

I found a job as a mechanic in a garage in Union City owned and run by a very smart Italian who taught me a lot about automatic transmissions and general repairs. He had a used-car business, which brought us a lot of work.

One day, after a couple of years, Steve asked me if I thought I could run the garage for three weeks so he and his family could vacation in Italy, where he was born. I said yes. When he returned, he had a pain in his chest and went to a doctor. They found he had lung cancer and removed one third of a lung. I continued running the shop.

Shortly after he healed and returned to work, I developed an infection under a little fingernail. As a cleaning tank to clean the transmissions we rebuilt, Steve had cut a fifty-five-gallon drum the long way, turned it on its side, and mounted it on a stand. We would then fill it partway with gasoline to wash parts. After a while, the gasoline would become quite dirty. That caused an infection.

I was out of work for two and a half days. After I returned to work, at the end of that first week back, Steve handed me my pay for the week; it was short two and a half days pay. I was shocked. I said, "Why am I short?"

He said, "You were out two and a half days!"

I said, "I will be looking for a new job!"

He said, "Wait, here are the two and a half days."

I said, "Keep it! If it was not in your heart to pay it, I don't want it!" I left!

We remained friends after that. Often, I would return to borrow his transmission jack to do a side job. It was necessary to leave Steve to advance my career.

Chapter 6

AAMCO

I got a job as a transmission rebuilder with AAMCO. There are three kinds of rebuilders: One may take a whole day and produce a transmission that might outlast the owner but will not make much money for the shop. Another may repair four to five a day, but half may come back. The third, and best of all, is the one who will rebuild two to three a day, which will create income and have a 10 percent chance of a comeback. I was among the latter.

The owners of the shop where I worked bought another AAMCO shop and asked me to manage it. I agreed. I also rebuilt some transmissions on the side. I managed this shop for five years and did quite well for them. One year I received an award for selling the most lifetime guarantees in one year. However, I found this was not for me, especially after realizing that when you can no longer do the physical work, there is nothing beyond. To pay the bills, we had to sell about twenty lifetime guarantees per week.

Chapter 7

ANGEL NUMBER 5, PATRICK M.

It was during one of those times when I went to Steve's garage to borrow his transmission jack that I met Patrick M., a CPA, who was a customer of Steve's. He saw me working and said, "You don't look like you belong here!"

After some conversation, he offered to give me a letter of recommendation to a friend of his who was the director of IBM's Service Bureau Corporation, a subsidiary of IBM and its education division. Patrick turned out to be my next angel. I had no idea what lay ahead!

Patrick did not tell me why he helped me; maybe he just had a feeling about me. I went to SBC and took a programming aptitude test. I was required to sign up for their IDP (Intro to Data Processing) course. I was one of four people out of twenty to pass.

I enrolled and was late for the first class, held by Joe B. He had binary numbers all over the blackboard. He said to me, "You have a problem," but fortunately, I did not have a problem. Not too long after I started working as a programmer, I was able to read and calculate in binary and hexadecimal as well as I could read English.

I passed the course and had to take another test to go on to the next course. I was one of five out of twenty to pass that test and go on. I signed up for assembly language programming. I was in heaven!

I'd found my niche in life! This stuff was better than any high I could ever get (I never touched drugs of any kind in my life). I passed! Assembly language was for me. I took these classes in the fall of 1968 and finished by December. I paid over eight hundred dollars for the classes.

At that time, I was working as a manager of AAMCO in Jersey City. I told the owners of my intentions. One said, "You are making a mistake." The other said, "You are doing the right thing! Get out of this business." The first owner would often refer to me as recalcitrant; the second became a friend and was a great guy.

I remember going with him to deliver a car to a customer. When he left the customer's house, he collapsed on the street. I helped him up and into the car, then took him back to the shop. I told my managers I would train anyone who applied for the management job to ensure a smooth transition. I found out, some years later, that my friend lost a battle with a brain tumor. I felt bad, as I liked him very much.

CHAPTER 8

CHANGING CAREERS

I searched for employment in the IT field for six months, taking several programming aptitude tests. One interviewer mentioned it would be best if I could do something about the condition of my hands, as they could be a turnoff to interviewers. Since I was still rebuilding transmissions at AAMCO for a living, my hands were never very clean. They also were peeling in various layers due to the solvents used to clean parts.

It was then I found Playtex Bluets rubber gloves, which allowed me to clean parts and keep my hands clean. They were thin enough to allow me to feel small parts and lasted a while before needing to be replaced.

I applied to and was turned down twice by IBM. Their reasoning was that I was making $10,000 a year as a manager but would have to start at IBM for $5,000 a year. They said that since I had a wife and two children and a house, I would have to work a second job, which might cause a problem with my first job.

When I applied to IBM for a third time, the interviewer decided to take a chance on me (at that time, a general equivalency diploma was acceptable). He hired me, and IBM placed me in SBC, the very place I took my classes. I was accepted under the stipulation that I did not work with machinery due to my double vision.

They had a printing service and placed me in the mailroom for one year to the day. I made three times the salary IBM paid me by rebuilding transmissions, but IBM never suffered due to my part-time work. In fact, in all modesty, I became an asset to IBM. By using my programming knowledge to write programs to run operations more efficiently, I saved them a lot of money in reruns of failed applications.

I worked third shift that first year. I spent most of my time taking printouts off the printer, separating them, and packaging them for customers. The first year was exciting, and although the work was not challenging, I loved it.

Three weeks after I started, SBC posted a notice on the bulletin board for a hardware class, which required an IDP prerequisite. I'd had that prerequisite before I joined SBC, and so I took the class. I had no idea it would bother my fellow workers. They did not have the prerequisite, so they could not take the class.

Almost all of them blackballed me for six months. Since we worked from midnight to eight, someone would take orders and go to Smiler's restaurant for lunch. No one would ask me!

There were two or three who did not blackball me, like Ziggy Kwiatkowski and Jim Miaki—good people who became my friends. But no matter; I was okay with the others too. My manager sensed the tension and asked me if I wanted him to talk to the others. I said no. They would come around in their own time.

I worked at SBC for one year to the day—May 31, 1969 to May 31, 1970. Then SBC was sold off due to a government mandate that IBM break up its monopoly. So, as it turned out, I just made it under the wire to find employment with a company like IBM.

A wonderful memory of working at SBC, which was at 1350 Avenue of the Americas in New York City, was that often I would see Moondog outside our building, sitting on one of the planters, drinking soup, year round. You could not miss him in his horned helmet, cloak, and Viking boots laced up. According to Wikipedia, Moondog was blind from the age of sixteen and lived in New York. He was known as "the Viking of 6th Avenue" and was an American musician, composer, theoretician, poet, and inventor of several musical instruments.

During that first year at IBM, I worked three jobs. On Friday at about six in the evening, I would go to sleep until 10:30 p.m. I would eat, shower, and shave, then race to IBM. It was okay to park on the street until eight in the morning. Then we had to move our cars quickly, as there was a tow truck waiting at the end of the block to tow anyone parked after eight.

I would then race home, grab a bite to eat, change to work clothes, and go to work at Lee Miles Transmissions from ten Saturday morning to two in the afternoon. There was a gas station in West New York, and the guy there would call me to rebuild a transmission he had removed from a car. I would pick up a rebuild kit and rebuild the transmission. This would take three to four hours.

I would then go home, shower, shave, and get dressed to join my brother and a couple of friends to go to Union City to have a couple of drinks. We would stay out until three in the morning on Sunday. This went on for a year. I also went to Rutgers Annex in Jersey City for two semesters, two subjects per semester that year.

Chapter 9

MARITAL CONFLICT

My wife, Janet, would often go to bingo or have some lady friends over to play cards. One night while she was at bingo, my son Timmy was playing with a ball in the house (it was winter and cold). The ball went behind the gas furnace, which was installed in the kitchen. The kids were very agitated, flushed, and too hot. We also had headaches and were irritable.

I leaned over the furnace to get the ball and smelled what seemed like carbon monoxide. I called the gas company, who sent someone over immediately. They shut the system down, stating that the flue pipe was blocked. When they left, I took the flue pipe apart and found it plugged solid with soot. I was able to clean it completely and turn the furnace on again. If I had not smelled the fumes, we might have died that night!

In 1970, my wife and I separated, then divorced in 1974. Janet and I had a great deal of stress between us, always arguing and yelling. We just grew apart. I think her biggest problem was listening to her friend who was extremely jealous of her husband to the extent that she caused him to leave his job. He said she cut up all his suits to get him to quit! She claimed he was seeing women in the office. She filled Janet's mind with the idea that I also was seeing women at IBM, although I vehemently denied it. Janet never believed me.

The stress got so bad that during one of our arguments, Janet told me to leave the house (as she had one hundred times before). I had to choose between staying for the love of our children or leaving to save them from the screaming arguments. I accepted her demand and left the house. I moved back to my mother's house for three months.

I met my second wife, Vivian, two weeks before I left Janet. After living at my mom's house for three months, I moved in with Vivian, a widow with five children. Her husband had died at thirty-nine from cirrhosis of the liver. Vivian's children ranged from nine to seventeen years old. We moved three times from 1970 to 1974 when I bought a house (a fixer-upper) in 1974 out of foreclosure.

Chapter 10

ANGELS 6 AND 7, ART B. AND SEYMORE R.

I was offered a position with IBM in operations at their 315 Park Avenue office products division as an operator. This office was also scheduled to close, since IBM OPD was completing a building in Franklin Lakes, New Jersey, where those who wanted to could relocate. While in OPD as an operator, I worked with Mike T., who helped me learn how to run a computer.

Mike was a nice guy who became my friend. He was very technical. Together, we created a procedure to load the night's production into the system, to be released when required, instead of manually typing each at the time it was to run. We also proved to management that two computers could share the same disk drive instead of each having its own, which was costlier.

Almost one year later to the day, IBM OPD opened Franklin Lakes, New Jersey. We were transferred as the first crew to work there. In SBC, I had worked third shift, midnight to eight. In OPD, I worked second shift, four to midnight. In Franklin Lakes, I was finally placed on first shift. Having assembler language experience, I started practicing coding in assembler.

Our director, Ron B., created a technical support position, to which he promoted my friend Mike. I continued as an operator. Management allowed me to practice writing assembler language programs. Soon after, I was promoted to a technical support position, assigned to systems support.

I couldn't believe it! Here I was, someone with a GED, working side by side with the elite—college graduates, master's degrees, doctorates! I worked with the programmers who helped create IBM's first online order entry system in Endicott, New York. One of them, Art B., was a very friendly person who had a tremendous amount of patience. He also taught me a lot about programming and became my mentor.

Art was another angel who worked with several of the other members in systems support at Franklin Lakes who were the developers of IBM's order entry system. He was a brilliant programmer who introduced me to control blocks in the operating system. I took to it like a duck to water.

My first program was designed to initialize scratch tapes. Applications would run sometimes for twenty-four hours, call for a scratch tape, and fail because an incorrect scratch tape was mounted. As it turned out, I discovered I was pragmatic and could find a problem and fix it. I wrote some programs to help operations run smoothly.

Another person for whom I have a great deal of respect and admiration is Seymore R. Sy taught programming at the college level. He could program in just about any programming language and had a great deal of patience. He helped me a lot with exits I was asked to program (e.g. sort exit, security exit, etc.). I admired these people who had multiple degrees, with their gentle mannerisms, patience, and composure. I aspired to be like them. I felt very humbled to be working with such great talent. It was a far cry from trying to start a car at night in a sleet storm, standing in slush up to your ankles or adjusting valves on a hot engine in ninety-degree heat, breathing burning smoke from a hot manifold.

After a year or two, I was promoted from operations to systems support as a systems programmer. I loved it! No one ever had to tell me what to do, since I always did more than was expected of me. I supported five MVS mainframes for fifteen years in a problem-solving capacity. As a system programmer, I had an opportunity to write tools to enable operations to run more smoothly, with fewer failures. Some of the programs I wrote were as follows:

- Copy tapes and erase extraneous data beyond the file, also skipping errors. Smith Kline and Beecham and Amtrak asked my manager if I could recover tapes that had data checks and could not be read. I copied the tapes and recovered all of them.
- Create preprinted labels for output tapes on production runs, eliminating the possibility of mislabeling tapes due to handwritten errors.
- Two sort exit programs: one modified the tape input records to an operating system disk sort (allowing the job to run much faster and sparing all but two tape drives when it ran) and the other changed records back to their original format.

Often, operations would call me to say that all systems were locked out. I would tell them that I did not look at the clock, so when I was out of time, tap me on the shoulder and take a dump of the system. Often, the problem would be a lost interrupt on a disk drive. I would give them the drive address, they would pop the plug to cause an interrupt, and systems would continue to run.

Chapter 11

REAL ESTATE OPPORTUNITY

I bought a four-bedroom townhouse out of pre-foreclosure in 1974. One of my sisters-in-law told me about neighbors who were having trouble paying for a house they owned in Jersey City. I looked at the house and spoke to the people on a Wednesday; they said they were going into foreclosure that Friday for $10,000. A friend of mine knew a lawyer who gave me a mortgage for the property. He represented both of us, the buyer and the seller. He suggested I add $1,000 to the price to allow the people to not leave empty-handed, which I did. He gave me a 9 per cent mortgage for $11,000, which I paid off in five years.

I put $20,000 into the house and cashed out in the mid-eighties for $129,000. I sold it in 1993 for $103,000. I completely rebuilt the house, adding a heating system, replacing the load-bearing beam, and then jacking it up two and a half inches. It also had a nine-by-twelve-foot extension that had settled thirteen inches in one corner. This was caused by the builders, who built the extension on clay, without a foundation.

I hired a carpenter to help me. We jacked it up and removed the rotted lumber on the side that had settled. I dug a trench eighteen inches deep (frost level for the area) and poured a concrete footing on the side and rear wall of the extension. We replaced the rotted studs. We could not jack the extension up thirteen inches, so the carpenter raised the floor joists on the second floor to level, one at a time.

Chapter 12

MINDFULNESS COURSE

In 1976, Vivian read an advertisement in the newspaper about a mindfulness course coming to the area. She said she would like to go. The course was the Silva Method, which is taught in many countries and languages around the world. It was created by Jose Silva, a Mexican in Laredo, Texas. Jose developed a method to teach his children how to improve in their studies. The course teaches you how to relax and meditate by going into an altered state of mind, where you can reprogram your subconscious.

The difference between the Silva Method and other forms of meditation is that once you are in an altered state of mind, you can take advantage of being able to communicate directly with your subconscious and reprogram it. Unlike the others where you relax, find your center, and repeat a mantra, in Silva we repeat affirmations like "Everyday in every way, I am getting better, better, and better" (quoting Emil Coi, a pharmacist in the 1800s); "I will always maintain a healthy mind and a healthy body"; and "Positive in, negative out!"

Since then, I have developed my mind for the better. I also developed two beliefs: "I will always be in the right place, at the right time, doing the right thing!" and "I will always get what I need when I need it!" It works all the time for me, whether I am looking for a parking space, getting gas, getting extra money when I need it, remembering things at the right time, etc.

Vivian and I attended the course together. Our first instructor was Lou O., who experienced what he taught. He mentioned he spent time with Tibetan monks, learning how to improve his mind and meditate. He told us he was in a motorcycle accident once, and as he was thrown into the air and hit the ground, he felt bones break and thought, "I feel the bones breaking, an experience I may never feel again," or something like that. The point was to experience the experience, whatever it is.

Silva instructors are trained in Laredo, Texas. Few went through what Lou went through. I am so glad he was our first instructor! Silva allows members to repeat the course in any country, as many times as they wish. A lot of the knowledge we gain comes from members who had experiences that sometimes are inexplicable.

Chapter 13

ANOTHER REAL ESTATE OPPORTUNITY

In 1978, I bought my mom's house, a Victorian built in 1892. My mom passed away in November 1973 and willed her house to my brother Dan, who lived with her until her passing. At that time, Michael, another brother, was living with Dan and our mother. Dan lived with Michael for five years, during which time he added a brick stoop and did some cosmetic work to the ground-floor basement, in which he lived and slept. Michael slept on the second floor but used the same kitchen Dan used on the ground floor.

After five years, Dan wanted to leave the house, so he offered it to me for $5,000. I searched city hall for a record of the first mortgage and found that in 1892, a $2,000 mortgage was taken out on the land (that had to be the first mortgage). After I purchased the house from Dan, I went to the house to see what had to be done. My brother Michael still lived there alone but did not work. I knocked on the door, but there was no answer. I knocked several more times; still no answer.

On one side of the house was an alleyway with a window to the bathroom and a pantry. I tapped on the windows; still no answer. I called out to Michael, but no response. Since Michael never drove a car and rarely left the house, I knew he had to be there. I listened and heard what appeared to be talking. I went up the stoop to the screened-in porch and opened a window.

It was near the end of day and getting darker. There were no lights on at that level. I went into the hall to the stairway leading down to the ground floor. Again, no lights. I went down the stairs. The ground floor hallway was totally dark. I found the light switch, but the bulb must have been dead.

I knocked on the living room door, but there was no answer. I opened the door, and the room was dark. There were two windows in the living room, covered with newspaper, through which the last light of day was providing a bit of light to the room.

In the far left corner of the room, my brother Michael was sitting in my mom's favorite rocking chair. He rocked slowly and muttered lowly, "Get out, get out!" He had a hammer in his right hand (think Jack Nicholson in *The Shining*).

I backed up to the door saying, "It's me, Mike, Terry. No problem, I'm going!"

The next day, I went to the police and told them I owned the house and needed access. They accompanied me into the house. I explained to Michael that Dan had sold the house to me. Since he was still living there, he naturally thought the house belonged to him. They took Michael away (not sure how long, probably overnight; no charges were filed).

Michael stayed in the house for ten years while I rebuilt it from the bottom up. He had been fired from Maxwell House after working there for many years. I think he was let go due to absenteeism or lack of punctuality. Mike was a gambler and a drinker. He waited too long to collect Social Security, so I applied to disability insurance for him.

He would never consent to see a psychiatrist, so I made an appointment with one and told him it was for his back pain, which he really did have from bowling. During the process, he was evaluated and diagnosed as a paranoid schizophrenic. He was eligible for disability (supplemental security income). He was prescribed medication, but I doubt he ever took it.

Chapter 14

ANGEL NUMBER 8, MIKE R.

I went to the building department and told them I was going to rebuild the house. The building inspector, Mike Regan, said he needed seventeen copies of architectural plans before I started. I went home, got a brown paper shopping bag, opened it up, squared it up, and drew a scaled drawing of the top floor: no water, just electrical, and no movement of walls. I rolled it up and took it back to Mike. He nearly fell on the floor laughing.

He turned to me and said, "Terry, just to the just, right!"

Then I nearly fell on the floor! That was one of my mom's witticisms! I never in my life heard anyone say that before or after. Makes me believe she was watching over me.

I got a basic contractor's license and went to work. I never let Mike down. I did much more than the building department would have asked of me. For example, the house was four stories tall, so I added a Z-shaped fire escape. Mike said, "That is not necessary, since it is listed as a single-family house."

I said, "I have to look in the mirror. I do not want someone to die by jumping out a window." I also built a fire-resistant room, complete with piped-in air, a fire door, and fire-retardant Sheetrock, as well as a sprinkler system and fire and smoke alarms.

I went through the house looking to see if there was anything of value, since Mom never threw anything away. There were fourteen rooms in the house on four floors. From the first floor to the third floor, there was furniture stacked up to the ceilings. I called two antique dealers to get an estimate; both said there was nothing of value in the house.

Then an old African American man (think *Sanford and Son*) came over and went through the house. He offered $150 for six chairs—all of which had a visible steel plate holding one of the sides of their backs with large screws (Mom's repairs)—and a bureau in my mom's bedroom. I said, "Give me $200 and take all the furniture." He declined.

I could not figure why he wanted those chairs. I found out sometime later while shopping in a used-door warehouse in Hoboken. While I was talking to the owner, he said, "Do you see that couple over there?"

I said, "Yes."

He said, "They may buy that fireplace set for $9,000."

I said, "Why so much?"

He said, "Because it's made from bird's-eye maple."

A light went off in my head! I remember seeing a label on the back of my mom's bureau that said it was made from bird's-eye maple. I thought, *Well, good for you, my friend. I am happy for you!* The old man probably came across a deal like that very infrequently.

I completely insulated the house, added two picture windows, changed all the other windows and all the doors, reduced the entryways from double doors to a single nine-light crossbuck door, added two heating systems and two hot-water boilers, and replaced all plumbing, water, waste, and gas pipes. I updated three bathrooms, two kitchens, two decks, and a coin-op laundry room, and added roof ventilation and reroofed. I installed cedar siding front and back. Except for a few times when my son and a couple of his friends would help, I did most of the work myself.

Once I removed the entire waste-pipe system (the soil stack was split in two lengthwise from the basement floor to the top floor), I replaced it all with black ABS plumbing. It was all complete, and then three people (including one inspector) told me ABS pipe was illegal in Jersey City, since when on fire, it produced toxic fumes. I tore it all out and hired a plumber to replace it with white PVC piping.

After the house was complete, the inspector who inspected the plumbing said, "You could have left the ABS." It was not illegal! What? Go figure!

Chapter 15

ANGEL NUMBER 9, CARMINE

I went to a TV repair shop in the neighborhood to get a TV tube. While there, I talked to the owner, Carmine. I mentioned I was rebuilding a house on Ogden Avenue and needed to find a licensed electrician to sign for permits to rewire and install new services to the house. Carmine said he was a retired maintenance person from the school system and had an electrical license. I asked him if he could sign and how much would he charge, since I would be doing all the work.

He said, "No charge. I will go with you to sign the permits." Then he said, "Do you know what you are doing?"

I said, "Yes. I am following the National Electrical Codes book."

He said he would check on me from time to time. I was off and running again.

I installed the service drop, which is the connection between the cable from the pole in the street to your house, which connects to your meter. The head of the service drop at the top was about forty feet from the ground. I had to take three cables (the size of a man's middle finger and capable of providing 200 amps to the building) and fish them through a thirty-five-foot-long, two-inch-wide galvanized pipe to a trough at the ground-floor level upon which the meters would be mounted. To do this, I had to drop a fish line down the pipe, then tie it at the second-floor deck to the cables (all three), then go downstairs and pull the fish line. This was tedious and involved a lot of back and forth: pull two inches, go upstairs and push two inches, go down and pull two inches, go up and push two inches, etc., for thirty-five feet. I installed one 100- and two 50-amperage sub panels. I completely rewired the entire house.

Carmine had to go to the building department again to sign up for the permits for another year. When it was finally time, Carmine came over to tie the service into the live wires from the pole. To help him reach the spot, I leaned a one-hundred-year-old wooden ladder from my second-floor deck to the house next door, which was across an alleyway of about forty inches.

As Carmine started to climb the ladder, I said, "Wait! I don't want you to risk your life for me. Tell me what to do, and I will do it."

Carmine said, "There are three cables that come from the pole. One is braided steel, without a cover; that is the ground. First cut that cable, leaving enough to reach your new cables and hook to a screw eye in the building. That will hold all the cables' weight. When you cut the cable, drape it under the ladder to avoid accidentally touching one of the other wires, which are live."

I followed his instructions.

"Now," he continued, "you can cut either of the remaining wires and connect to the new wire."

When I was through, I had to connect each new and old wire with a bronze U-bolt and triple-wrap each connection with first rubber tape, then adhesive tape, and finally electrical tape. Carmine said I did a good job.

After the electrical service was installed and tested, the inspector came over and inspected everything, including the two furnaces I installed. He said, "I never saw so many outlets!"

I said, "The code book said every five feet."

He passed everything except one small thing: a jumper across the water meter. The house ground wire was connected to the plumbing system, so a jumper was needed across the meter, since the meter has paper gaskets on each end for input and output. Everything got a green tag, including the two furnaces I installed.

Chapter 16

STILL REBUILDING MOM'S HOUSE

The house was so neglected that the roof leaked through all floors down to the ground floor basement. I gutted the house completely. Fortunately for me, Jersey City wanted people to improve their properties, so they offered dumpsters for free. They gave me six and hauled them away when full, no charge.

One dumpster contained the remnants of a four-foot blue stone wall surrounding an extension I removed at the back of the house. Blue stone rocks are very dense and heavy. If you struck one with a hammer, it would almost ring, they were so hard.

I had a friend, whose name escapes me, who lifted weights (he reminded me of Mr. T, the actor). He worked for a mutual friend in the business. I hired him for two hundred dollars a day to carry those rocks to the dumpster in front of the house. I could not pick up even one of the stones. It took him two days to complete the job and fill the dumpster. When the tractor came to remove the dumpster, the load was so heavy the front wheels of the tractor rose off the ground. Eventually, the driver was able to get the dumpster loaded onto the tractor.

When Mom bought the house, she had to argue with the city to have it changed to a single-family house to lower the property tax. (It must have been a rooming house when first built, judging by the layout). When my work was complete, I had to reverse it again to a two-family. I'm sure it must have been the first house in the area, since when I removed the plaster from the first floor hall, there was a doorway leading to the alleyway that had been sealed off. It would have been impossible for anyone to go down a flight of stairs to that alleyway of forty inches! It took three years to complete the electrical system and twenty years to finish the house in my spare time.

Sometimes I hired my son and his friends to help me. I installed nine thousand feet of Sheetrock in the house, and taped and spackled a lot. But most of the taping and spackling was done by a woman, Cynthia R., a little bit of a thing. I paid her ten dollars an hour. I gave her a key, and she kept track of the hours she worked. I don't think she was even five feet tall. She would change into her shorts and go to work. I remember thinking her shorts looked like they were Barbie Doll shorts, they were so small! But man, could she spackle. She was recommended by a counterman at a lumberyard where I bought materials.

Once, when I was living there with my third wife, Marie, and my grandson, we went to McDonald's for a bite to eat. I sent my twelve-year-old grandson to ask Michael if he wanted anything. He asked for a hamburger. We got him a hamburger, fries, an apple pie, and a malt. When my grandson went to his door and handed him the food, he went ballistic! I thought he was going to harm the boy! He yelled at Timmy, "I did not ask for all this. Just a hamburger. Take it away." Then he slammed the door in Timmy's face.

After ten years of having him living in the house I was renovating, I got Mike into subsidized housing, with food stamps as well, in the Journal Square area, which was a place Michael always loved. That was around 1988. Michael passed away in 1998 of colon cancer. He lay in his room for five days until someone in the building complained of an odor from his apartment and notified police. I visited Michael from time to time, but he was extremely antisocial.

I intended to keep the house and possibly live in one of the apartments. Unfortunately, the area was going downhill rapidly.

I started the rebuild (not to be confused with restoration, since I changed its character) in September 1978 and completed the work in 1998. I rented the upstairs two-story apartment for $1,200 a month and the second-floor studio apartment for $600. I also made an apartment on the ground floor for my brother, Michael, at no charge.

I put $90,000 in material into the house. I cashed out of the house in the mid-1980s for $149,000, then sold it in 1998 for $130,000 to an African American woman, her daughter, and her aunt. Where did I get all this money? Loan after loan after loan from my IBM credit union and withdrawals from my 401k.

Chapter 17

LIFE WITH VIVIAN

Vivian was working in a lamp factory when I met her in 1970. Sometimes she would leave work with burns or cuts on her arms from the glass or fires at her job. I felt bad for her and urged her to go to school for something, anything. She went to Katherine Gibbs secretarial school and graduated. She found a job working for a real estate attorney, who was very patient. However, he was rather strict, so I urged her to leave and go somewhere else.

She found a job in New York as a secretary, but again wound up with a rough manager. I felt bad for her, since she enjoyed Manhattan so much. She would take her lunch to a beautiful lobby with a waterfall and an eating area and enjoy her break. She was very happy working in that area.

Vivian was a wonderful person and a great wife. We enjoyed life together. About twice a year, IBM would send me to a technical conference to network and bring back any information that might benefit our installation. I would take Vivian with me, since the room was paid for anyway. I only had to pay for her airfare, meals, and entertainment. She liked to gamble a bit and enjoyed Las Vegas. She was lucky and liked to play 21.

Sometimes she did not join me but drove me to Newark airport and continued to Atlantic City. Once she ran up her winnings to $1,100. They offered her a room, which she took. The next day, she gave back

$300 and quit. She went home with $800. She never gambled to the extent that it caused a problem. She always kept her wits about her.

Vivian's mother lived in Branchburg, New Jersey, which we visited often. Since I was once an auto mechanic, I would find myself repairing someone's car while everyone else was relaxing and enjoying themselves. I did not mind, since I felt I was helping someone.

Once, when I was walking to the house, I noticed a different car in the driveway: a Ford. When we went into the house, Vivian's sister and brother-in-law were there. I asked about the car; they said they just bought it (used). I don't know why, but I said, "The car is okay, but the chassis is shot!" This was without looking at the car at all.

I went outside to look at the car, crouched down on the passenger side, and looked under. I could not believe what I saw! The chassis, just below the passenger door, was almost completely rusted away. I don't know how I knew but did not question it.

In 1982, we were watching a panel show on TV where they were talking about breast cancer, and they mentioned how women should check themselves for lumps. I asked Vivian if she ever checked herself, and she said no. I urged her to get checked, which she did. She was diagnosed with stage 1 breast cancer. I felt so bad for her.

When she was three years old, she was playing with matches and set her dress on fire. She almost lost her life, suffering burns from her navel to her neck. She lost her left breast due to the burns. Her torso was covered for six months from the burns, which left her with scars over the front of her torso.

Now, doctors performed a radical mastectomy of her right breast as well as radiation therapy. Vivian was told by her oncologist that they had removed all the cancer. However, our family physician said she should get chemotherapy anyway, since it only takes one missed cell to metastasize. Vivian elected not to take chemotherapy.

Her aunt had breast cancer at the same time and had the same surgery and radiation but did elect to have chemotherapy. She is still alive today. Maybe Vivian would be too if she had made the same decision.

Chapter 18

TRIALS AND TRAGEDIES

After having smoked cigarettes since I was twelve years old, I wanted to quit. I wanted to gain more wind power and more energy. Toward that end, I attended an introduction to a Smoke Enders seminar. Throughout the introduction, their emphasis seemed to be that smoking was a choice, so I may just as well condition myself to "choose not to smoke cigarettes."

Another aid to being able to quit was one day while at the counter of a drugstore purchasing cigarettes, a gentleman behind me said in a low gravelly voice, "They're no good for you!" He had gauze over the hole in his throat from where he had his voice box removed.

This hit me like a brick. That was it! At 7 a.m. on April 8, 1985, I had my last cigarette. I was determined not to smoke another cigarette for the rest of my life. I treated cigarette smoking like alcoholism. If I put one between my lips, I would go back to smoking. I have not touched a cigarette since then.

Fast forward to April 10, 1986. I came home from work to find my twenty-three-year-old son Timmy going into an ambulance in a wheelchair. I followed them to the hospital. The doctor had a lot of trouble finding a vein in Timmy's arm to give him an intravenous. I had no idea what was going on.

Instinctively, I started reprimanding Timmy. "What did you do?"

Timmy responded, "Not now, Dad! I'm dying!" What was he talking about?

Timmy was moved to another room. His mom and sister, Terrilin, followed him to that room. I was going through a lot of mixed emotions: anger, sadness, hurt, disappointment. I had been having a lot of trouble with Timmy, and this seemed to be the straw that broke the camel's back. I was in the middle of rebuilding two houses by myself, dealing with Timmy's antics, and juggling four stepsons and a stepdaughter, two jobs, etc.

Shortly after Timmy was moved, I was still in the triage area when I had an overwhelming feeling of sadness that brought me to tears. While I did not see Timmy die, I knew he was gone. Timmy passed away on April 10, 1986, at 8:30 p.m. The doctors did not tell me what happened, just that he had double pneumonia.

When I went to the funeral home to arrange Timmy's burial, the director told me the casket had to be sealed. I said, "Why?"

He said, "Because he had AIDS!"

"What!" I exclaimed. I had no idea! I never knew he was on drugs of any kind. It seemed he shared a needle with a friend of his who had AIDS. These were some of the first victims in 1985.

I did not start smoking again. I thought that if I could get through the loss of my only son, there would be nothing in this world that would make me smoke cigarettes again. I am still free of cigarettes.

In 1988, Vivian's cancer returned and metastasized to her bones. It was so sad—like she could not get a break. I cashed out on the two houses, paid off the loans, and set about putting Vivian in business. She had read about Toning Table machines that women used to exercise their bodies. We met the salesman and purchased two sets of machines for $50,000.

I leased a row of law offices above a local five-and-ten store that occupied a space of about fifty by one hundred feet. I gutted the offices, had an electrician upgrade the electrical service to add 400 amperes to power fourteen machines, and created a fifty-by-one-hundred-foot salon with exercise equipment, a body wrap system, and a nail service.

Vivian managed it. I came after work and managed the books and payroll. Including the cost of the machines, it cost me $135,000 total. That came from the cash-out of the houses. The salon lasted eleven months. When I realized I was subsidizing the business with my salary, I had to close the doors.

Several things contributed to the failure. One was a very large, heavy man who was the brother of a nurse who was a customer. She also brought some of her nurse friends to join. The man, who signed up for a body wrap, was so heavy we could not weigh him.

When someone joined, we would take tape measurements of their body at different points before a body wrap. I could not in all conscience let the girls who worked for me take those measurements (also because he had sores on his body), so I would take them. He took exception to that! He would tell risqué jokes to the girls, which embarrassed them. I asked him to stop. He would not. I told him if he continued, he would not be allowed to stay. He left and took his sister and all her friends with her.

Another problem was that a Work Out World center opened directly across the street and took some of our customers. The final reason it failed was that my customers wanted tanning tables installed. I said no, because I was convinced they caused skin cancer. Fortunately for me, the landlord, who was subleasing the space to me for a five-year period, had a heart and let me off the lease, which would have cost me $80,000 for the remainder of my sublease. Another angel!

Vivian passed away on New Year's Day, 1991, at 11:30 a.m. The hospital had her on life support, with tubes all over. At one point, the doctor said the two sections of her heart were beating independently of each other. She needed a pacemaker. I approved the surgery.

Shortly after, her oncologist said her body was shutting down. We should remove the life support. I had to agree, although I did not want to. Vivian's entire family was there, but she was in a coma and not communicable. We were all in tears. She was loved very much by all.

When Vivian passed away, I had her buried in the Somerville, New Jersey, area where her entire family lived (except her children and me). They would visit her more than I might have. I let her mother pick the cemetery, plot, and headstone. I kept Vivian in my mind.

Chapter 19

LIFE WITH MARIE

Five months after Vivian's passing, my friend Frank asked if I would like to come over for a small pool party. He said a friend of his wife, Lois, would be there. I attended and met Marie. We chatted a bit and seemed to get along well.

For July 4, 1991, Frank invited me to another pool party and said Marie would also be there. Marie and I spent a lot of time talking. She mentioned that she worked for New York Bell Telephone and was a member of the Telephone Pioneers, an organization that did many charitable things throughout the year (feeding the homeless, working with Habitat for Humanity, Santa to hospitals, etc.).

I mentioned to Marie that I had two sets of exercise machines that I needed to get rid of; sets of these machines were going for as little as $600, since no one used them anymore. I had fourteen machines—two sets. Marie said she would talk to her Pioneer chapter president to see if they could use the machines. We made a dinner date for the next day, when she would have word from the chapter president.

On July 5, Marie and I had dinner at the Light House in West New York, New Jersey. Marie said they would love to give the machines (I had no intention of selling them) to a senior citizens' home in the Bronx. I said I would pay to move them to the home.

We never came off that date. I moved in with her that night.

I called my muscular friend and asked him if he and another friend would like to load the machines onto a truck. These machines were made of thick steel and padding and weighed about two hundred pounds each. These guys had to carry them down two long flights of stairs. Ordinary movers would not have been able to do this.

I was able to donate the second set to a senior citizens' home in South Amboy. Seniors benefited from these machines because the machines moved their muscles for them without effort on their part. This brought blood to their joints and helped them. The salon could not survive on seniors alone; it needed more.

Amazing guy, Frank! He introduced me to all three of my wives! Thanks, Frank! Marie and I married in November 1991 and moved into the Victorian I was rebuilding to finish it. Michael was still living there.

I had built a laundry room on the ground floor, next to Michael's apartment. Every time he heard Marie washing clothes, he would open the adjoining door and socialize with Marie. He loved Marie and she liked him too. This was Michael's only social life. Sad he was so antisocial, as well as schizophrenic.

For most of Marie's life—since she was eighteen years old— she had worked for all of the telephone companies in Manhattan (AT&T, New York Bell, Bell Telephone, etc.). One year, one of the executives in Marie's office held a Christmas party in his apartment in a skyscraper in Manhattan. While walking around the apartment, I looked out a window to enjoy the view. What I saw was incredible! A few floors below us, outside a penthouse apartment in a building across the street, was a fully assembled vintage Sopwith Camel airplane (think Snoopy's plane) on a runway with running lights! Of course, it could never take off from that runway, as it was too short. But what a conversation piece!

I spent twelve years volunteering with Marie and the Telephone Pioneers. They awarded me Pioneer of the Year that first year because of the machines I donated. We would feed the homeless in Manhattan with the Coalition for the Homeless, run by a man named Frazier (we did this at least once a year). A group of Pioneers would get together and make about a thousand sandwiches for the homeless. The coalition provided an equal amount of oranges, milk, soup, and Italian rolls. Some of us would collect coats, blankets, wool socks, hats, and gloves. Once my car had so many in the back seat that they touched the ceiling.

One year we bought a couple of hundred thermal tops, which the homeless enjoyed so much, as it was winter. Frazier had two routes: one would go north, the other south. We followed in our car (under bridges, cardboard cities on the waterfront, the 83rd Street rotunda, etc.).

One year, a young African American lady came to our truck shivering and asked for a coat. Marie had a poodle-cut coat in the trunk that her mother gave her a while ago and that was starting to get a little ratty. She said, "Get the coat!"

I said, "Marie, I don't think we should give her that coat!"

Marie said, "Get it anyway!" She gave it to the young lady, who had nothing but a short leather blazer. You would have thought we gave her a mink coat. She danced around showing off the coat. She was happy! At that time, I also gave up a car blanket I had in the trunk to a shivering Latino.

Another time, at the 83rd Street rotunda, there were people, even small families, lying on the ground in the winter. One man asked us for wool socks. Unfortunately, we had none. I asked him, "What happened to your socks?"

He said, "They smelled so bad, I threw them away." He was barefoot, on a concrete floor, in the winter. I gave him a couple of wool hats and told him to wear them on his feet. He did and was happy to have them. How sad to see so many people living like that. Some even went on line in wheelchairs.

We would do Christmas parties at McDonald House in Manhattan and soup kitchens. Pioneer members dressed as Santa Claus went to nursing homes to cheer residents. We worked with Habitat for Humanity, built a bocce court for a Home for the Blind (for visitors), and did some work for Paul Newman's Hole in the Wall ranch for kids, including painting twenty-two buildings and erecting a steel building. We would go anywhere we were needed. These were the best years of my life. Marie was the most giving, loving person I ever knew.

Chapter 20

BUYING A CONDO

After we sold the Victorian, we moved to an apartment in Kearney, New Jersey, for a year (we were still working but planned to retire soon). I talked to Marie and said if we stay here, we will be throwing money away. It would be four years before I could retire at sixty-two years old. But if we bought a house, we could save money.

Marie found a condo in Millburn, New Jersey, for $85,000. It was beautiful! It was on the ground floor, with a backyard that was like a park and the Raritan River running fifty feet from our bedroom window. Taylor Park was only a block away, and there was a ShopRite next door to our village, a quaint downtown a couple of blocks away, and the Millburn Playhouse a quarter mile away. Perfect!

In the winter, the river would freeze, and young people would ice skate on it, right outside our large picture window—our own Currier and Ives scene! I upgraded the kitchen with new cabinets and floor tiles. I also built a closet in the bedroom. The apartment had 550 feet of space, but we managed very well. We even had people over.

One Christmas, we had three couples over for dinner and entertainment. One couple had a video they took in Milan, Italy, of a fashion show for 3x to 6x ladies; the couple had a boutique in Bayonne, New Jersey, where they manufactured clothing catering to large-size women. They were invited to judge the fashion show in Milan.

When we put the video in our TV, it took a while for a picture to come on, as it was an older, tube-type TV. After they left, and a couple of days later, we received a thank you from one of the other couples, a woman who had a chiropractic business, and her husband, who had a turnkey medical office computer application and employed seventy-five people. They included with their thank-you card a check for three hundred dollars and a note stating, "Here! Buy another TV!"

Chapter 21

1995: DANNY'S SEVENTIETH BIRTHDAY

Our nieces held a seventieth birthday party for Danny, their uncle, at the Ramada Inn in Carteret, New Jersey. My brother Kenny and I were Danny's only living siblings. Kenny could not make it, so that left me to make a toast. I thought about it for a while but could not think of one that would be appropriate.

On the day of the party, when it came time to toast Dan, I toasted with the following: "A birthday toast to me brother Dan, whose intelligence you see, is less than this man! Though he goes to extremes, to excel me, he dreams! Ah, but 'tis I who dreams to be better than!"

Dan was in fact very intelligent and well read. I could never win an argument with him. I was kidding him when I said that. However, I had no idea where that limerick came from! It was not the first time that happened to me, nor the last.

On October 2, 1998, at 8:30 p.m., my first wife Janet passed away.

Chapter 22

RETIRING AT SIXTY-TWO

We stayed in Millburn, New Jersey, until I retired on December 31, 1999. There was so much panic over what might happen with the turnover to a new millennium—the infamous Y2K problem. As a programmer, let me explain that.

All programmers knew that January 1, 1900, was a Monday. So who needed to enter the century of 19 in their code? At that time, programs in assembler were limited to 4K (a K is 1024 bytes). So even saving a byte (1 character) for the century was necessary. But when you came to 12/31/1999 and went to 01/01/2000, the year is now 00—less than 99! Control blocks on tape, disk, and in memory only provided one byte for the year, nothing for the century (they compared the year for one byte, not two).

As it turned out, it never created the problem, though many thought it would. Since I wrote programs that included that logic and did not account for the century, I elected to retire. We vacationed in Italy and watched the ball drop with Marie's cousins. Prior to retirement, I was asked by one of my fellow programmers at IBM if I would like to contract to companies with him, such as banks, that were paying a lot of money (my friend suggested six hundred dollars per hour) to scan programs for the Y2K code. I said, "No, I am going to retire."

We sold the condo for $120,000—a $35,000 profit. We bought a home in a small development in Brick, New Jersey; it had always been our intention to move to the New Jersey shore. We paid $150,000 for a two-story home with three bedrooms. The community had a large outdoor pool and a clubhouse.

I bought a used pickup truck, and every Friday, I would pack it up and move it to the new home, then stay for the weekend. Eventually, I moved all the small stuff myself. Once the move was complete, I sold the pickup truck. I upgraded the kitchen with new cabinets and floor tile, as well as other upgrades.

Chapter 23

MARIE'S BACK PROBLEM

Marie had back pain caused by a car accident in 1978. She had two herniated discs in the lumbar area that caused her great pain. She went to a chiropractor often, sometimes twice a day. She also had a friend who had a practice in North Jersey who sometimes came to her house to adjust her.

When we lived in the Victorian in Jersey City, we found a yoga instructor, Yolontha, who held sessions in Hoboken. It was hatha yoga and helped Marie quite a bit. After a year and a half of yoga, Marie felt much better and was in a lot less pain. In fact, Marie only visited a chiropractor once a month.

In the summer of 2003, we were visiting Marie's cousins in Rome, Italy. They took us to their summer home in Saint Andrea, Calabria. The home was on a mountain on a switchback road. We were returning from dinner with their friends in a car their daughter borrowed from a neighbor, who lived on the mountain also, but two switchbacks below. I thought she would drive us to her home, but she did not.

Marie suffered a lot walking up those two switchbacks, and I could not help her. I asked Marie's cousin to drive her to the house, but she walked ahead, ignoring us. I thought she was angry at her mother for having to spend her time showing us around while we were there.

It was then that Marie decided to have an operation on her back. We found the best doctor in New York, who said he could help her. Before the operation, Marie had to go to another doctor to prepare her for the operation: bloodwork, checkup, chest X-ray, etc. At the time, we did not know it, but the radiologist who read the chest X-ray sent a report to the prep doctor saying there was an infiltration in the lower lobe of her left lung.

The prep doctor never told us what the radiologist found. We do not know whether the surgeon was told or not. Marie had the operation. This was in December 2004. Around May 2005, Marie started to feel good, with hardly any back pain.

Chapter 24

MARIE'S BAD BREAK

Marie started to feel what she described as a catch in her left side, near her ribs. Early in September 2005, we went to our family doctor, who ordered an X-ray every week for four weeks. Finally, he sent us to a pulmonary doctor, who performed a bronchoscopy on her left lung and found fourth-stage lung cancer in October.

We went to Sloan Kettering in Manhattan, New York. The oncologist said the cancer was non-small-cell carcinoma and was treatable. He said chemo and radiation were necessary, but an operation was not possible.

The first cocktail they tried was a triple solution, which almost killed Marie; she had trouble breathing and felt as though a weight was on her chest. By the time they finished chemo that day, we were the last ones out of that section of the building, very late at night.

Marie received chemo and X-rays until January 2006. On the last visit to Sloan Kettering, the doctor called me while Marie was in triage. He said Marie's body was shutting down and there was nothing more they could do.

Marie went home for a while. I got her a hospital bed, which only lasted about two days. Then we took her to hospice, where she passed away the next day, February 2, 2006, at 8:38 a.m. I was at her side when she passed away. She had a tear in her left eye.

Marie was the love of my life. I will never forget her. We loved each other very much and enjoyed a very close relationship. She loved my daughter and grandchildren so much and treated them as if they were her own. My eldest granddaughter, Tara, dreams about Marie often. I was so happy to have spent part of my life with her and so proud to have been her husband.

Sometime before all this happened, Marie and I decided to move out of our development. We went to a town meeting where we found the city was going to open two new parkway entrances and exits that would pass right by our pool fence. They intended to move a bus station behind our fence as well. I told Marie we should move, and she agreed.

We looked at Four Seasons on Shorrock Street in Lakewood and decided we would move there. We never made it together, but five months after Marie passed away, I moved to Four Seasons, a complete retirement community. I've met some nice people there. They have many activities, indoor and outdoor pools, complete gym, golf, and many different clubs. I belong to the Chorus and the Rock and Roll Club, where we enjoy ten dances a year with well-known groups performing. The Chorus performs a Memorial Day program, a holiday program for Christmas/Hanukkah, and a summer and fall project (the last was a tribute to Sinatra).

Although I am still alone, I hope to find someone who can share my life. Meanwhile, I still enjoy life at Four Seasons. I also wrote lyrics to a song, which I hope to sell once I find an appropriate melody.

Chapter 25

LOSING MY LAST TWO SIBLINGS

On September 17, 2013, my brother Kenny passed away. Marie and I used to visit Kenny and his family in Pennsylvania around the holidays. Kenny would take us to a tree farm to cut down a Christmas tree.

One year, when tying the tree to the roof of my car, Kenny remarked that the twine I used did not look like it was strong enough. I said it was, not to worry. Then, on Route 80, the wind and speed proved Kenny right. The twine broke, and the tree flew off the roof and crashed onto Route 80.

I pulled over, and before I could recover the tree, a truck ran over it and broke it in two. I scrambled between traffic to remove the big pieces from the roadway. We bought another tree locally where we lived.

Kenny had some medical issues. He passed away after a brief hospitalization. I still miss him and the times we had together: dual guitars, singing, visits, parties!

On June 2015, my brother Daniel, my last living sibling, called our niece Barbara and said he felt he needed to go to the hospital. Dan had two bouts of colon cancer in his life, and now he was having his third. He also had lung cancer, which we were not told until after his death.

He was in the hospital a while when he decided he did not want to be stuck with any more needles. He refused treatment. He was moved to a hospice facility in Brick, New Jersey, near me and a couple of our nieces. Dan was eighty-nine years old (born in 1926). He stayed in hospice until August 5, 2015, when he passed away at 10:30 a.m.

Dan did not have a will (he died intestate). The surrogate court assigned me to be his administrator. When I went to the surrogate court, they told me I would have to obtain a surety bond. I said, "Where?" They told me there was a real estate office right next to their building in a small mall. I went there and found DansKin Realty. What? Was Danny watching over me? Dans Kin? Okay, I got the surety bond.

Then I had to empty his apartment. Dan was a collector and threw nothing away. I had three of our nieces come to his apartment to see if they wanted anything. After they left, I had the job of emptying the apartment of furniture, books, dishes, shelving, etc.

Dan also collected coins, stamps, and memorabilia—nothing that was worth anything, except for some Carson City silver dollars. Before he passed away, he said I should be sure to get a good broker to buy the collectibles. Dan thought he had a lot of valuable items. Unfortunately, he was buying the wrong collectibles (such as Fleetwood stamps, now worth five to ten cents per stamp, and silver coins that were supposed to be uncirculated but in fact were not). I gave the stamps to a niece for her kids to look at and keep.

I found a coin dealer on the internet, Robert A., who said he would come over and look at the coins. When he knocked on the door, I said, "Hello, Robert!"

He said he was not Robert but his brother Daniel. *What?* I thought. *Are you playing with me, Dan?* That was weirdo number two from Dan!

Daniel looked at all the coins and said they were not as good as they were represented. He bought the Carson City silver dollars and left.

Later, I was in a local strip mall going to the post office when I noticed a jewelry store that advertised that it bought gold and silver. I stopped in and the man said, "Bring me what you have, and I will see what they are worth." I brought what was left in two small bags. I opened one bag and showed him a brochure from a company where Dan bought the coins in the 1970s. There was a picture of a man on the brochure. The jeweler said, "That is me!"

What? Again? The jeweler was appointed in the 1970s to head a committee to grade coins. His name was Stephen A. The coins had gone full circle. He worked for a lawyer who sold Dan the coins.

Chapter 26

ALONE AGAIN, BUT NOT ALONE

So, as you can see, I am living quite an interesting life, filled with wonderful people to whom I owe a great deal. I will never forget any of them. They passed through my life and I through theirs. I would not trade one minute of it for all the tea in China, which is why I titled this book the way I did: *I Had My Cake and Ate It Too! Thanks to My Angels!*

May God bless all of you! There is nothing better than loving what you do and doing what you love. It has been said that, "If you love what you do, you will never work a day in your life!" You will never know until you take that first step. I did and look how life turned out for me. Some may say, "But you lost so many people you loved!"

I would say, "I am grateful for the time I had with them, however long it was!" I hope all of you find what I found in life.

Printed in the United States
by Baker & Taylor Publisher Services